Pope Francis

Brian Doyle

Illustrated by Derry Dillon

Published 2018
Poolbeg Press Ltd

123 Grange Hill, Baldoyle
Dublin 13, Ireland

Text © Poolbeg Press Ltd 2018

A catalogue record for this book is available from the British Library.

ISBN 978 1 78199 851 9

Cover design and illustrations by Derry Dillon
Printed by GPS Colour Graphics Ltd

IHS
MISERANDO ATQUE ELIGENDO

This book belongs to

Early Days

Jorge Mario Bergoglio, Pope Francis, comes from Argentina in South America. He is the first ever pope from the Americas and the first pope to be born outside of Europe since the 8th century. He was born on the 17th December,1936, in Buenos Aires [Good Winds], the capital city of Argentina. His first language was Spanish, the main language of Argentina, though his family came from Italy. Jorge is a Spanish name – it is pronounced 'Horhey' and is the Spanish for 'George'.

Jorge's grandfather was an Italian winemaker. Mario José, his father, was an accountant for a railway company and lived in the Piedmont region of Italy. Jorge's mother, Regina Sivori, was born in Buenos Aires to a family of northern Italian origin. Jorge's father emigrated in 1929, from Italy to Argentina, because of the rise to power of the Italian dictator, Mussolini, who started his own political party, the Fascists. Mussolini wanted to make Italy a great power and invade other countries. He supported Adolf Hitler, the German leader, during World War II.

In September 1929 the family left their ancestral home, which had a tile above the door with the words: *Signore, benedici chi entra in questa casa* [Lord, bless whoever enters this house]. They set sail for Argentina on the ship *Giulio Caesare* [Julius Caesar] and after a long voyage they finally reached their destination, Buenos Aires. Jorge's grandmother Rosa wore a fur coat, in the lining of which she had hidden Italian lire from the sale of their property in Italy. This money would give them the opportunity to start a wonderful new life and to buy a new home in Argentina.

Jorge was the eldest of five children. He had two brothers, Alberto Horacio and Oscar Adrian, and two sisters, Maria Elena and Marta Regina. Maria is eleven years younger than Pope Francis and is the only one of his family still alive.

Jorge was very close to his grandmother Rosa, who spoke Italian. He spent a lot of his childhood talking and listening to her. Rosa taught him many things about the Catholic faith, including the stories of many of the saints. She taught him how to pray and Jorge decided that he would make sure to pray every day! He learned Italian from her. Jorge's father would not speak Italian to him because he wanted his son to be fluent in Spanish, the language of their new country, Argentina. Jorge said of his grandmother Rosa that she was 'the one who had the greatest impact on me. It was she who taught me the Catholic faith'.

Soccer, Music, Love and the Tango

Jorge's family lived near their local church and school in Buenos Aires. His family went to Mass every Sunday. In his local school, he is remembered for jumping up and down as he repeated his times tables! He was a great reader. He enjoyed playing basketball. He loved playing soccer with his friends, but he wasn't very good at it! His favourite soccer team is still San Lorenzo [St Lawrence] in Buenos Aires and he loves to watch soccer as often as he can. Jorge was and still is very interested in music. He spent many hours in his home with his mother listening to classical music and opera on the radio. He has said 'It was just the most lovely thing'. His favourite composers include Mozart, Bach and Beethoven.

When he was a young teenager he fell in love with a girl called Amalia Damonte. He wrote her a note saying *'If you don't marry me, I will become a priest'* and put it in her hand when he met her in the street. When her father found the letter, he was furious and Amalia wasn't allowed to see Jorge any more.

Then, when he was 17, Jorge had another girlfriend and they used to go dancing together. Argentina is famous all over the world for a special dance called the tango and Jorge was a great fan. He danced it whenever he could.

The 21st September 1953 was a very important day in Jorge's life. He was a student of chemistry at an industrial college and that evening he set out for the dance hall with his friends. On the way they passed some hungry children begging in the street and this bothered Jorge. When they reached the dance hall he turned around and went back to the local church to pray. He then went home and told his parents he wanted to become a priest and spend his life helping others. His father was delighted but his mother cried. She was disappointed as she knew he was clever and she'd thought he had a great future ahead of him as a lawyer or a doctor.

In 1957, when he was 21 years old, Jorge became seriously ill with pneumonia. Unfortunately, antibiotics were not available at that time and he had to have part of his right lung removed. Thankfully this didn't prevent him from having good health in the future.

While he was a student, Jorge had several jobs to help him earn some money. He worked as a janitor and a bouncer in a local bar in Buenos Aires! He obtained a diploma in Chemistry and worked as a chemical laboratory technician before he entered the seminary to become a priest.

The Priest, the Bishop and the Cardinal

On the 11th March 1958, Jorge joined the Jesuit Order as a student priest. The Jesuit Order was founded by St Ignatius Loyola of Spain and some others in 1534. A few days before his 33rd birthday Jorge was ordained a priest on the 13th December 1969 – and his mother asked for his blessing at the end of his ordination.

Jorge really enjoyed his life as a priest. He loved meeting all kinds of people, rich and poor alike. He liked to chat and to listen to them. He helped many people who had all kinds of problems in their lives. He visited the sick in their homes, in hospitals and on the streets. He used to say, 'My people are poor and I am one of them'. Father Jorge was humble but also a person who was not afraid to speak his mind!

Part of his work at that time was helping young Jesuits on their journey to becoming priests. In 1973 he was very surprised to be appointed as the Superior of the Jesuit order in Argentina and Uruguay, which meant that he was responsible for all the Jesuit priests in those countries. He worked hard at this job for six years.

An Argentinian army commander, Jorge Videla, became the dictator of Argentina from 1976 to 1981. During his rule, some 30,000 people disappeared or were killed by the country's army during what became known as 'The Dirty War'. Father Jorge stood by his people, helping and defending them against the soldiers. He even gave his passport papers to a man who looked like him, so the man could escape from Argentina. He was brave to do such a thing. It was a very difficult time for the people of Argentina and for Jorge.

In 1980 Jorge spent three months learning English in Milltown, Dublin, Ireland. This time in Dublin gave him a chance to rest from the stress of the troubles in Argentina. As well as Spanish and Italian, Jorge speaks Latin, German, Portuguese and English. He also speaks some of the Piedmontese dialect from his parents' home in Italy.

In May 1992, Pope John Paul II appointed him Auxiliary [assistant] Bishop in Buenos Aires. After three years, he became Archbishop of Buenos Aires. Even though he could have lived in the Bishop's Palace there, he made the choice to live in a simple apartment. He cooked meals not only for himself but also for others. 'Well, nobody has died yet from my cooking!' he said. He chose not to be driven in taxis or a big, fancy car. Instead he walked, took the bus or the underground! He wanted to live a simple Christian life, visiting the sick, the disabled, the poor and helping in the soup kitchens where the poor and hungry came to be fed. He gave a great example of what it meant to be Christian. He chose not to wear the fancy clothes of the Bishop of Buenos Aires and wore the simple clothes of a priest.

Then Pope John Paul II made Jorge a cardinal in February 2001. He was now called Cardinal Bergoglio. A cardinal's job is to help elect a new pope, to attend meetings called by the pope and to help organise and manage the Catholic Church. Although this was a very high-ranking position, he continued to live a very simple and humble life. But he did have his own Coat of Arms! He now had many extra duties but he made time to visit his priests when they were sick and elderly. Giving them a special phone number, he told them to ring him at any time, day or night, if they needed to speak to him.

Then, in April 2005, he went to Rome to take part in the Conclave to elect a new pope at the Vatican, which is a tiny independent state in the middle of Rome where popes live and work. It is the smallest country in the world!

The result of the election was amazing: Pope Benedict XVI was elected but Jorge, the humble cardinal from South America, was the runner-up!

Habemus Papam! [We Have a Pope!]

Pope Benedict XVI resigned in February 2013 because he felt that he was too old and unhealthy to continue as pope. Jorge travelled on an economy flight to Rome to join with his fellow cardinals in the selection of a new pope. He had bought a return ticket as he never expected to be elected.

On the 13th March 2013, the second day of the Conclave, white smoke was seen coming out of the chimney of the Vatican buildings to show that a new pope had been chosen. The crowds erupted in applause and cheering, and the bells rang out. Then the announcement was made from the balcony of St. Peter's Basilica: *'Habemus Papam!'* which is Latin for *'We have a Pope!'* Cardinal Jorge Mario Bergoglio was elected! No one was more surprised than Jorge himself! He became the first pope in history to replace a living pope – normally the old one dies first.

Rather than the usual blessing of the people by a new pope, he asked them to pray for him. 'Let us say this prayer, your prayer for me, in silence,' he told the people. He didn't use the traditional platform to speak to them because he didn't wish to be considered more important than the cardinals who were standing beside him. He wore simple white instead of the traditional colourful papal robes, and a simple metal cross. He said to the 150,000 people gathered in St Peter's Square that his fellow cardinals had gone 'almost to the end of the world to find him'. As the crowd cheered and sang with joy he said to them: 'Good night, and I wish you peace. We will see each other soon.'

His sister Maria was hoping that Jorge would not be elected because she wanted her brother back in Buenos Aires! But she cried tears of joy when she heard the good news! She said that he would be a humble pope, a pope of love, especially love for the poor and love for the truth.

As pope, Jorge chose the name Francis. This was in honour of the famous St Francis of Assisi of Italy, a man of peace and of the poor who lived a very simple life and had a great love of animals and respect for the environment.

His Coat of Arms as Cardinal Bergoglio was now converted into one with a pope's pointed mitre (hat) on top. The Latin motto means *'having mercy and choosing'* — Pope Francis means Jesus had mercy and chose him.

Still a Simple Man

In the year that he became pope, Francis was named as *Time Magazine*'s 'Person of the Year' because of the huge influence he had on world affairs during such a short space of time. But he still clung to his simple way of life as much as possible.

After his election, he asked the Argentinian people not to come to his inauguration but to give their money to the poor. He rang his dentist in Buenos Aires and asked him to cancel his future appointments. He cancelled his newspaper order. Returning to his hotel, he paid his own bill. He chose not to live in the official papal residence but to live in an apartment in the Vatican guesthouse. He was now a citizen of three different countries: Argentina, Italy and the Vatican. He wore plainer vestments when saying Mass instead of the fancy robes and jewelled hats worn by the popes who came before him. He chose not to wear the traditional red shoes but to wear his old, worn-out black shoes instead!

He also bravely chose not to use the bulletproof Pope Mobile. He described it as a 'glass sardine can' because it would stop him from really meeting people. He says that if he is shot and killed it doesn't matter at his age!

Even though he doesn't ride a motorbike, he was given a Harley-Davidson as a present, but instead of keeping it he signed its fuel tank, sold it and raised almost €300,000 which he gave away to help homeless people.

Pope Francis enjoys simple pleasures like music and reading. He is a fan of J.R.R. Tolkien and even talked about the journeys of Bilbo and Frodo in *The Hobbit* and *The Lord of the Rings* in a sermon about life being an ongoing journey of hope!

Tweet, Tweet!

He may like simplicity but nevertheless Pope Francis is very much a man of the modern world and embraces technology. When he became the first pope ever to address a joint meeting of Congress in the United States of America in 2015, he even had his own 'emojis', made in honour of his visit. He uses Twitter to communicate his message to people all over the world. He tweets to over seven million Twitter followers on a frequent basis. He tweeted that he likes sweets and chocolate very much, that words without actions are empty and that people should love and help one another. If you feel like sending Pope Francis a tweet, you can, by contacting him at Pope Francis@Pontifex to receive words of wisdom from him on your Twitter page.

Feliz Cumpleaños! Buon Compleanno!
Happy Birthday!

On their birthday people usually spend their day going to the cinema, an amusement arcade or on a special trip. What did Francis do in 2013 on his 77th birthday? He visited sick children in the children's clinic in the Vatican! The sick children sang 'Happy Birthday' to him and they presented him with a lovely white-and-yellow cake, the Vatican colours. They also presented him with Sibila, a beautiful white dove, as a birthday present. A dove is a symbol of love and peace. Pope

Francis was surprised, excited and delighted! He had a pet parrot when he was much younger. On his return to the Vatican he had another party and invited destitute and homeless men to come and join him! He reminded people that Jesus had done the same when he shared meals and kept company with people who were looked down on and ignored by everyone. On his 81st birthday he celebrated by sharing a 4-metre long pizza with sick children from the same clinic! Cool dude! 25,000 people came to St. Peter's Square in the Vatican to sing 'Happy Birthday' to him! Wow! That's a lot of people to have at your birthday party!

Treno dei Bambini – The Children's Train

Pope Francis adores children. In May 2015 he invited 200 girls and boys to come by train to the Vatican. They were the children of women and men in different prisons in Italy. And in May 2016 roughly four hundred children arrived from southern Italy – he had invited them to have a party with him. They came from different ethnic, cultural and religious backgrounds. Many of them were migrants and refugees who had made the dangerous crossing of the Mediterranean Sea in small boats from Africa, hoping for a better life in Europe. They had a wonderful party and great fun with Pope Francis. In 2017, following an earthquake in central Italy, Pope Francis invited around 400 children from the area to have a party with him. What a great friend to have, don't you think?

A Man of Compassion

Pope Francis is full of compassion for suffering humanity, past and present. In July 2016 he visited Auschwitz, the Nazi-German concentration camp in Poland, to honour the 1.5 million people who were killed there during World War II. Most of those were Jews, many of whom were children. This was his very first visit to the terrible Nazi camp. He chose to pray in silence there and met twelve Auschwitz survivors. He wrote these words in a visitor's book in Auschwitz: '*Lord, have mercy on your people. Lord, forgive us for so much cruelty.*'

His compassion drives him to make many trips abroad to highlight particular problems. He went the Greek island of Lesbos to visit refugee camps and brought three Muslim refugee families from war-torn Syria back with him to live in Rome. He travelled to Armenia and spoke out against the mass killing of Armenian civilians during World War I.

In January 2018, he visited Chile and Peru in South America. He met 4,000 people from various tribes in the Amazon rainforest. He asked that these people, their homes and the rainforests be respected and protected from selfish governments whose only wish is to destroy their unique way of life.

Sometimes his trips are more enjoyable, like when in 2017 he visited Fatima in Portugal, where Catholics believe that Mary, the mother of Jesus, appeared to three shepherd children in 1917. About 500,000 people from all over the world gathered there to honour the three children. Pope Francis announced that brother and sister Francisco and Jacinta were now to be known as saints. Their sister Lucia will be canonised in the near future.

Pope Francis will visit Dublin, Ireland, in August 2018 to attend the World Meeting of Families. As well as saying Mass in the Phoenix Park, Dublin, he intends to meet people who are experiencing poverty, homelessness and loneliness in the city. He is also planning to visit one of the city's prisons.

Many Religions – One Father

Religious leaders from around the world met in Japan, in 2017, to pray for peace. Pope Francis sent a letter asking those present to work, pray and help to bring about peace, friendship and dialogue between the world's different religions. In November he spoke to Muslim, Buddhist, Hindu, Jewish and Christian leaders who had gathered in Myanmar. He said that they had 'one father' and that they were all 'brothers'. He said they should live in peace and respect and understand each other's religious beliefs and differences.

In September, in South Korea, he met with leaders of Korea's seven major religions. He called on them to speak peaceful words against war and violence in the world. He asked them to respect each other's faiths and beliefs, to respect the dignity of human beings, to work hard at putting an end to poverty and hunger and to respect the world's climate and environment.

In December he met with Protestant leaders from 129 different nations to discuss religious freedom throughout the world. He said that Christians should be at peace with each other, fighting climate change and corruption, helping victims of the many natural disasters affecting the world and helping each other to stop Christian persecution.

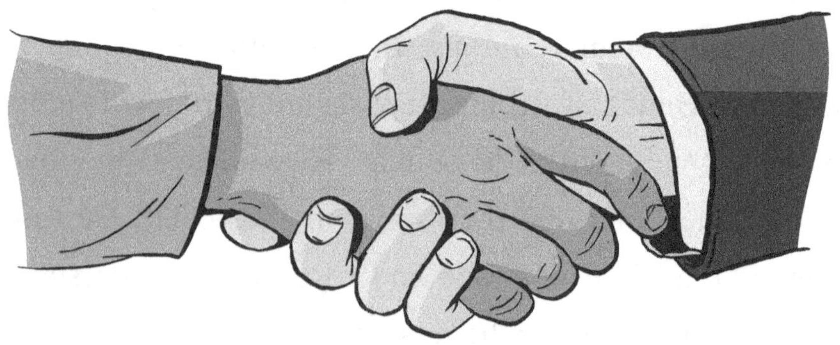

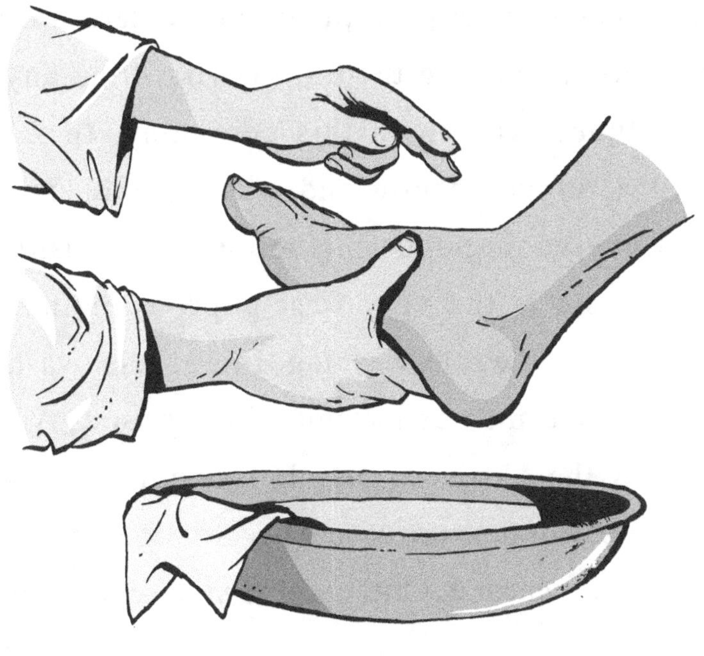

Washing Feet

Jesus washed the feet of his twelve apostles at the Last Supper, the night before he was crucified. This was to show his apostles that he had come to serve them and that we are all equal. The ceremony of the washing of the feet is usually done in church on Holy Thursday, in memory of that event. Pope Francis, however, likes to show his loving nature by doing it in prisons and refugee camps. In 2013, he washed the feet of twelve young people in a juvenile prison. There were two young women among them – the first time any pope has included women in this ceremony. In 2016 he visited a refugee centre and washed and kissed the feet of twelve migrants, including three Muslims and a Hindu. He is the very first pope to include non-Christians in the foot-washing. In 2017, he washed the feet of twelve men and women in a prison. After the ceremony the prisoners gave him two dessert cakes, a handmade wooden cross and fresh vegetables grown in the prison garden. One good turn deserves another!

The Five-Finger Prayer

Pope Francis loves to pray. He says many different kinds of prayers of course, but he has own special Five-Finger Prayer! Long before he became pope, Francis used this unique and personal prayer to help him pray for other people. The thumb is the nearest to you and it reminds you to pray for those who are closest to you: your parents, brothers, sisters and friends. We use the index finger to point at things or people, so remember to pray for teachers and others who instruct us, guide us and heal us through life. The middle finger is the tallest one: pray for those who are world leaders, presidents, governors and all those in authority – they need our prayers and support. The ring finger is the weakest finger: pray for those who are helpless, sick and poor in the world. Sometimes they can feel forgotten about and lonely. The smallest finger reminds you to pray for yourself. Maybe you might say this special prayer sometime!

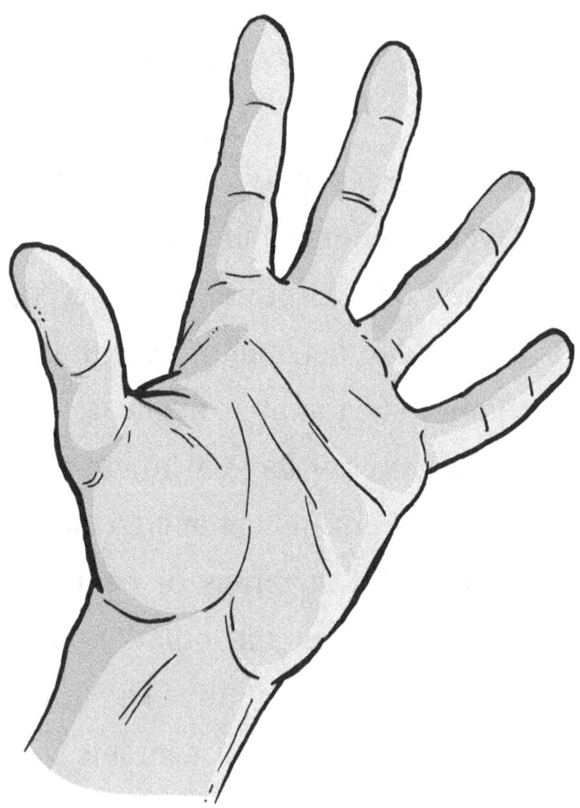

Pope Francis and the Environment

Pope Francis says that the earth, our home, is beginning to look more like a great pile of filth, filled with rubbish! We are destroying creation, our forests, our soil and polluting our skies and seas. We should take care of our earth as we take care of our homes. He even wrote a special document, called an encyclical, asking the world to listen to the cry of the earth and the cry of the poor. Climate change is destroying the world, he says.

The natural environment is being polluted by man's selfishness. Thousands of species will no longer live on land and in the sea because of pollution caused by human beings. Clean water, clean air and sufficient food are basic human rights that are not available to everyone in the world. He implores us to help the needy, stop global warming, love and respect the earth and to stop being wasteful, greedy, polluting and selfish. Let us hope that the world's leaders listen carefully and act quickly to save the world's environment! Well done, Pope Francis!

A Final Message!

Pope Francis wants all people to be peacemakers each day – in their lives, in their families, in their cities, in the whole world and to work daily to better their environment, their communities and themselves.

GLOSSARY *(alphabetical order)*

accountant: someone who keeps financial records

ancestral: belonging to a person who was in someone's family in past times

antibiotics: drugs to cure infections

archbishop: a bishop of the highest rank.

assassinated: killed for political reasons

bouncer: someone whose job it is to stop troublesome people from coming into a bar or party or force them to leave

canonised: someone very holy declared to be a saint by the Catholic Church

citizen: a person who is a member of a particular country

civilian: a person who is not belonging to the police force or the army

classical: part of a long, formal tradition and so of lasting value

coat of arms: a special shield that is the sign of a family, university or city

conclave: a private meeting where discussions are kept secret

dialogue: discussion

dictator: a leader who has complete control in a country

diploma: a document given by a college or university to show a person has passed an exam

document: an official paper that gives information

emigrated: left a country for good

encyclical: a letter from the Pope to Catholic bishops, about Church positions on an important subject

environment: the natural world OR the surroundings or conditions in which a person, animal, or plant lives

ethnic: associated with a certain race of people

Fascist: a person who believes a country should have a very powerful leader and control by the state, where opposition is not allowed

global: involving the whole world

humble: not thinking of yourself as better than other people

inauguration: formal ceremony introducing a person into an official job

indigenous: naturally belonging to a particular region or environment

influence: the power to change or affect someone or something

janitor: a caretaker or doorkeeper of a building

joint: shared or made by two or more people or groups OR point where two structures are joined (like bones in the body)

juvenile: relating to a young person not yet an adult

lire: Italian money

migrant: a person who travels to a different country or place, often looking for work

nationality: the right to belong to a particular country

ordain: Make someone a priest OR order something to happen

Order: a society of monks or nuns living according to particular rules

origin: beginning or cause of something

persecution: unfair or cruel treatment for a long time

pneumonia: an illness affecting the lungs

pollute: to make something unclean and harmful to people and animals

refugee: a person who has to leave their country to escape war or persecution, or some other disaster

seminary: a school for training priests

St: short for Saint OR short for Street

sufficient: enough

superior: better or higher in social position than others

symbol: a thing that is used to represent something else

technician: a person whose job is about the use of machines in industry, medicine, etc

Timeline

1936: Born in Buenos Aires, Argentina, to an Italian immigrant family

1939 – 1945: World War II

1947: Juan Peron elected President of Argentina. His wife, Evita, becomes
First Lady of Argentina.

1948: Mahatma Gandhi assassinated in New Delhi, India

1955: Military uprising in Argentina

1957: At age 21, Jorge has an operation to remove part of his lung due to an illness

1958: Enters the Jesuit Novitiate

1960: Makes his first vows as a Jesuit priest

1963: President John F Kennedy assassinated in Dallas, Texas

1973 – 1979: Superior of the Jesuits in Argentina for six years

1978: Pope John Paul I elected and dies after 34 days in office
Pope John Paul II is elected

1981: Pope John Paul II wounded by a gunman in Vatican Square.

1982: War between Argentina and the UK over the Falkland Islands

1992: Jorge appointed Auxiliary Bishop of Buenos Aires

1993: European Union founded

1994: The end of Apartheid in South Africa

1998: Jorge installed as Archbishop of Buenos Aires

2001: Created a Cardinal by Pope John Paul II

2005: Pope John Paul II dies

2008: Barack Obama elected President of the United States of America

2013: Cardinal Bergoglio elected Pope and takes the name Francis

Some Things to Talk About

1. What nationality were Pope Francis' parents?

2. In which country was he born?

3. What was his first language?

4. How did his family influence him in becoming a priest?

5. Name the languages Pope Francis speaks

6. What were the things that Pope Francis enjoyed doing as a young man?

7. What jobs did he have before he became a priest?

8. Who founded the Jesuit Order of priests?

9. Did Pope Francis enjoy his life as a priest? Why?

10. How did he show that he was a brave man?

11. Was he a humble man when he was a Bishop in Argentina? How do you know?

12. Why did Cardinal Jorge go to Rome in April 2005?

13. How can young people help to make the world a better place?

14. How can you be a peaceful person?

15. How can you help to make your environment cleaner?

16. Where does Pope Francis live now?

17. List three things that Pope Francis did immediately after he was elected Pope.

18. Why do you think he choose Francis as a name?

19. What is Pope Francis' motto on his coat of arms?

20. What kinds of things does Pope Francis do on his birthdays?

21. Would you agree that Pope Francis is a good man? Why?

22. Which questions would you like to ask Pope Francis if you met him?